Guide for Catholics
Beliefs of the Church

George A. Lane, S.J.

John Powell, S.J.
Theological Consultant

LOYOLAPRESS.

CHICAGO

LOYOLAPRESS.

3441 N. Ashland Avenue
Chicago, Illinois 60657
(800) 621-1008

ISBN: 0-8294-0845-2

04 05 DataR 10 9 8 7

Contents

Nihil Obstat
Reverend Charles R. Meyer, S.T.D
Censor Deputatus
August 18, 1995

Imprimatur
Most Reverend Raymond E. Goedert, M.A., S.T.L., J.C.L.
Vicar General
August 21, 1995

1 What Catholics believe about God

Catholics believe that there is only one God. They understand God as pure spirit, the creator of the universe. Catholics believe God is a Trinity. *Trinity* is a word that describes the mystery of three persons existing in one God: God the Father, God the Son (Jesus Christ), and God the Holy Spirit. God is the beginning and the end of creation. All things and all persons are meant to return to God in and through Jesus Christ.

Trinity

The Trinity has always existed. The Father, the Son, and the Holy Spirit are equal in every way. St. Patrick once compared the Trinity to a shamrock. The Trinity (like the shamrock) is of one substance. Each person of the Trinity (like each leaf of the shamrock) is distinct yet connected to the other two. Within the Trinity the Father begets, or generates, the Son. The Father and the Son together breathe forth the Holy Spirit.

The Trinity desires to live within us. The Father loves us very

much. He wants us to be close to him. For this reason God sent the Son into the world. Jesus invites each of us to share the life of God, by becoming one with him through faith and baptism. If we do this, we share his life and in his relationship with the Father. When we receive the Holy Spirit in baptism we become one with Jesus in sonship, which makes the indwelling of the Trinity possible.

2 What Catholics believe about Jesus

Identity

Jesus is both God and man. Sometimes he is called the God-man. He possesses both divine and human qualities. Jesus is God's son, the second person of the Trinity. He is also Mary's son. While remaining fully divine, he became fully human. Jesus was human in every way, but he did not sin.

Jesus* is the way we say the Greek name *Iesous. *Iesous* is Greek for *Yeshua.* The Hebrew name *Yeshua* means "God saves."

Christ* is the English version of the Greek word *christos.

Christos has the same meaning as *mashiah.* The Hebrew word *mashiah* means "anointed" or "the anointed one." When we call Jesus "the Christ" we are saying that he is the messiah.

We pray to Jesus so that he will pray to the Father for us. If we pray "in the name of Jesus," Jesus has assured us that the Father will hear us. It is the Holy Spirit who prompts us to pray. We direct our prayers to the Father, through the Son, with the Holy Spirit.

Jesus brings us into communion with God. Through Jesus we share God's life, the life of the Trinity. The human race enjoys a positive relationship with God, and eternal life is our destiny.

Birth

Incarnation **is a word that describes the mystery of God, the second person of the Trinity, becoming fully human while remaining fully divine.** The Incarnation and the Trinity are mysteries. Mysteries are truths revealed by God. Mysteries can never be understood entirely.

Jesus was born of the Virgin Mary. He was conceived by the power of the Holy Spirit. His father is God. His mother is Mary. Mary was a virgin when she gave birth to Jesus. She remained a virgin throughout her life.

Mission

Jesus came into the world to break down the barrier that existed between God and people. The barrier was the result of original sin, which refers to an act of Adam, the first man. It affects all human beings. Only Jesus and Mary escaped this alienation from God. Jesus becoming human and dying on the cross broke down the barrier. People were reunited with God. His death saves us from eternal death, from sin, and from the devil.

The Beatitudes are eight statements made by Jesus that tell us about true happiness:

Blessed are the poor in spirit for theirs is the kingdom of heaven.

Blessed are those who mourn for they shall be comforted.

Blessed are the meek for they shall inherit the earth.

Blessed are those who hunger and thirst for what is right for they shall be satisfied.

Blessed are the merciful for they shall obtain mercy.

Blessed are the pure in heart for they shall see God.

Blessed are the peacemakers for they shall be called children of God.

Blessed are those who are persecuted for the sake of what is right for theirs is the kingdom of heaven.

Jesus did three things that formed the core of his ministry. He preached the coming of the Kingdom of God, he healed the sick, and he expelled demons from people's bodies. Jesus began his public ministry when he was thirty years old. It lasted for three years until his death on the cross.

Demons are spiritual beings who harass humankind. They do not have bodies. Demons were created by God and were once good angels. They became evil through their own fault. They are referred to in the Bible. In Jesus' time, people believed that sickness, disease, and natural disasters were caused by demons.

Satan is the leader of the demons. The name *Satan* means "adversary." When Jesus came back to life, he weakened the power of Satan, or the devil, forever.

The twelve apostles were Jesus' closest followers. They were companions of Jesus. After Jesus' Ascension into heaven, the Holy Spirit empowered the apostles to teach every nation about Jesus and to proclaim the Good News of God's Kingdom. The Spirit also empowered the apostles and their successors to lead the Church.

We refer to Peter as the first pope, or bishop of Rome.

He was one of the apostles closest to Jesus. Jesus made him the leader of the apostles and the leader of the Church. Peter was head of the churches in Antioch and Rome.

The Last Supper was a meal that Jesus shared with his twelve apostles the night before he died. The Last Supper was probably a Jewish Passover meal. It was the first Eucharist. At the Last Supper Jesus gave the apostles his body to eat and his blood to drink. His body and blood were given to them under the appearance of bread and wine.

Death

Jesus was crucified. To crucify is to put to death by
 binding or nailing hands and feet to a
wooden cross. Crucifixion was a form of
capital punishment. Jesus was nailed to a
cross. His death was slow and painful. A
crucified person dies because the weight of
his suspended body eventually causes him
to loose control over the muscles that allow
him to breathe.

Jesus did not have to die. He died because he chose
to be obedient to the Father. Jesus' death
was part of the Father's plan to reunite us
with himself.

Jesus was killed by the Romans. He was sentenced to
 death by the Roman procurator (governor)
Pontius Pilate. The Romans had invaded and
continued to occupy Palestine. Palestine
was Jesus' homeland. Jesus was a popular
religious leader. He awakened the people's
desire to be free. The Romans viewed him as
a threat to their rule.

**After Jesus died his soul descended into, or journeyed
to, Sheol (hell).** *Sheol* is the Hebrew word for
"underworld." The ancient Israelites believed
that the underworld was located in the
middle of the Earth. They believed that it
contained the souls of all those who had
died. As Jesus left the underworld he took
the good souls with him.

Hell is the abode of the damned. It is the eternal
punishment that awaits evildoers when they
die. Their greatest punishment is that they
never will see God. Though Catholics
believe hell exists – something to which the
Scriptures refer – we do not know with
certainty that any particular person is there.

Resurrection

The Resurrection refers to Jesus' coming back to life.

Three days after Jesus' death, his soul was
reunited with his body. He came back to
life. His soul and body were glorified. This
means that Jesus never had to die again.
He had a different kind of body. He did not
have to eat or sleep. He could even pass
through walls and doors (John 20:19).

**After Jesus came back to life, he remained on earth for
"forty days."** This was the Jewish way of
saying "a suitable amount of time." While
on earth Jesus appeared to his mother and
disciples, continued to teach the apostles,
and worked miracles.

Ascension

The Ascension refers to Jesus' returning to heaven. Jesus'
 glorified body and soul rose into heaven forty
days after his Resurrection. In heaven, Jesus is
lord of the angels and saints. He sits at the
right hand of the Father, reigning in glory.

**After Jesus ascended into heaven, he sent the Holy Spirit to
his followers.** We celebrate Jesus' sending of
the Holy Spirit at Pentecost. Jesus continually
prepares a place for each of us. He also
intercedes for us—if we ask Jesus for help, he
will ask the Father to help us.

Heaven is being in the presence of God. When Jesus—who
was one of us—ascended to the right hand of
the Father, he was in heaven. Heaven also
refers to the dwelling place of God and
God's angels. We believe that the righteous,
or souls of good people, are with God in
heaven.

Purgatory is a state or place of purification. It is intended for
persons who are basically good but not quite
ready to enter heaven after they die. Our
prayers and good works can help them enter
heaven sooner.

**The Second Coming of Jesus will occur at the end of
the world.** The glorified Jesus will return in the
company of his angels. He will reward those
who have done good and reject those who
have done evil. The first coming of Jesus
occurred at the Incarnation.

Angels are spiritual beings who comfort humankind. They
 do not have bodies. Angels were created
by God. They are referred to in the Bible.
They carry out God's commands. Sometimes they serve as messengers. Angels also
protect people. At baptism, it is believed
that a guardian angel begins to watch over
us. The Archangel Michael is the leader of
the angels.

3 What Catholics believe about Mary

Mary is the Mother of God. She gave birth to Jesus who is God. Jesus is the Son of God (the second person of the Trinity) and the son of Mary. Sometimes Mary is called *Theotokos,* which in Greek means "God-bearer".

The doctrine of the Immaculate Conception affirms, or teaches us, that Mary was preserved from original sin. From the first moment of her conception, she was free from the stain of sin –including original sin – and remained so forever.

The doctrine of the Assumption affirms, or teaches us, that Mary was taken up into heaven body and soul by God. This occurred when her purpose on earth had been fulfilled. We do not know whether she ever died.

We pray to Mary so that she will pray to God for us.

We pray especially to her because she is close to Jesus. We do not worship, or adore, Mary. Catholics worship only God. We venerate, or revere, Mary because she gave birth to Jesus.

Mary is an instrument of God whom we can imitate. Mary is the Mother of the Church and our mother. Without Mary, Jesus would not have been born. She said "yes" to God's plan to send the Son into the world.

4 What Catholics understand to be the Tradition of the Church

The Tradition of the Church is comprised of Scripture and the Church's teachings over the centuries, particularly about the sacraments.

Scripture

 Scripture is the Word of God written down for our instruction and our salvation. It is the revelation of God's own self and of God's plan for our salvation in Jesus. The Word of God can be found in the Old and New Testaments.

The Old Testament is a collection of forty-six books. These books can be divided into three subject areas: the Law, the Prophets, and the Writings. The writing of the Old Testament began seven hundred to eight hundred years after the death of Moses. The Old Testament was written mainly in Hebrew. Parts of it were also written in Aramaic and Greek. The Old Testament is the name that Christians give to the bible of the Jews. Jewish people refer to their bible as the Holy Scriptures or the Hebrew Bible.

The New Testament is a collection of twenty-seven books.
There are four gospels: Matthew, Mark, Luke, and John. The Acts of the Apostles has been called the second volume of Luke. There are twenty-one letters. Seven of these letters definitely were written by St. Paul. The Book of Revelation is an apocalypse. An apocalypse is a book about the end of the world. The writing of the New Testament began about twenty years after the death of Jesus. The oldest New Testament in existence was written in Greek.

God inspired men and women to write the Old and New Testaments.
 The Old Testament tells the story of how God created the world and its inhabitants and how God guided and redeemed the Jewish people from the consequences of sin. *To redeem* means "to free, or to save, people from sin." The New Testament tells the story of how Jesus' life and death redeemed us.

Throughout the Old Testament God worked to save the chosen people. God called Abraham to be the father of all believers—first the father of the Israelites and later the father of Jesus' followers. The Israelites were slaves of the Egyptians for four hundred years. God called Moses to lead them out of slavery to the Promised Land. When Pharaoh and his army pursued the Israelites, God "parted the Red Sea" so that they could escape to freedom. Jews call their deliverance from slavery the Exodus, which they celebrate each year at Passover.

During the Exodus, God gave Moses and the Israelites the Ten Commandments:

God said: I am the Lord your God, who brought you out of slavery:

You shall have no gods except me. . . .

You shall not speak the name of the Lord to misuse it;

Keep the Sabbath day holy;

Honor your father and your mother;

You shall not kill;

You shall not commit adultery;

You shall not steal;

You shall not testify falsely against your neighbor;

You shall not covet your neighbor's wife;

You shall not covet your neighbor's possessions.

God's giving of the Law took place on Mount Sinai.

God called David to be a just ruler of the Israelites. God promised him that his descendents would rule forever. During his reign, the Israelites made Jerusalem their capital (around the year 1000 B.C.E.). The kings who followed David were corrupt. God's people imitated their ways and ignored the Law.

The Babylonians captured the Israelites and forced them into seventy years of slavery (around the year 600 B.C.E.). The years that the Israelites spent in Babylon are called the Babylonian Captivity, or the Exile.

The Israelites wondered why they came to be enslaved. Isaiah, Jeremiah, Ezekiel, Daniel, and the other prophets spoke to them on God's behalf. The prophets told the Israelites to worship only YHWH (Yahweh), the one true God. They reminded the people of their destiny and told them that a savior would come to deliver them. Eventually, God's people returned to their homeland (Judea). They were known as Jews from that time forward.

Sacraments

A sacrament is an action, a physical sign, in and through which God touches a person. God's touch conveys grace, forgiveness, strength, and life to a person.

The seven sacraments of the Catholic Church are baptism, confirmation, Eucharist, reconciliation, anointing of the sick, holy orders, and matrimony. Baptism, confirmation, and Eucharist are sacraments of initiation. The sacraments of baptism, confirmation, and holy orders leave a permanent mark on the soul. We call this mark a "character." The sacraments provide a way for us to keep in touch with God throughout our lives.

Baptism begins our initiation, or entrance, into the Church.

Through the sacrament of baptism we experience spiritual rebirth. Baptism gives us a permanent sharing in the priesthood of Christ, which we refer to as our baptismal priesthood. Baptism also gives us a permanent membership in the Church, the people of God. Baptism cleanses us of original sin. (It cleanses adults of original sin as well as mortal and venial sins.) At baptism the priest, deacon, or lay person immerses us in water or pours water over our head. We are baptized with the words, "I baptize you in the name of the Father, and of the Son, and of the Holy Spirit." The word *baptism* comes from the Greek word *bapto,* which means "to dip or to immerse."

Confirmation continues our initiation into the Church.

Through the sacrament of confirmation our spiritual life is strengthened. At confirmation the bishop or priest lays his hand on our forehead and anoints us with chrism (blessed oil). We are confirmed with the words, "Be sealed with the gift of the Holy Spirit." At confirmation we receive the Seven Gifts of the Holy Spirit: wisdom, understanding, right judgment (counsel), courage, knowledge, reverence (piety), and wonder and awe (fear) of God. The word *confirmation* means strengthening.

Eucharist completes our initiation into the Church. Through
 the sacrament of the Eucharist we receive
the spiritual nourishment of the Body and
Blood of Christ. At the Last Supper, Jesus
blessed bread and wine and gave them to
his disciples. Referring to the bread, he said:
"Take this, all of you, and eat it; this is my
body which will be given up for you."
Referring to the wine, he said: "Take this, all
of you, and drink from it. This is the cup of my
blood, the blood of the new and everlasting
covenant. It will be shed for you and for all,
so that sins may be forgiven. Do this in
memory of me." Jesus said the bread was
his body and the wine was his blood. He
spoke about his body and blood as an
offering that was about to be sacrificed.

By speaking in this manner, Jesus actually
anticipated (foresaw) the sacrifice of his
own life on the cross. When we celebrate
the Eucharist, we do more than reenact the
Last Supper. We also reenact Jesus' sacrifice
on the cross. The bread and wine actually
change into the Body and Blood of Christ.
This change occurs during the consecration.
The word *eucharist* comes from a Greek
word that means "thanksgiving."

Reconciliation heals, or repairs, our relationships with God and the Church.  Sin causes a separation between God and a person. It also causes a separation between human persons.

Through the sacrament of reconciliation the sins that a person commits after baptism are forgiven. Before receiving this sacrament, we must be sorry for our sins, we must want to be forgiven, and we must be determined to avoid sinning in the future. The priest then gives us the absolution, the forgiveness of Christ and the Church.

He also gives us a penance. A penance is something we do or say that shows we have turned away from sin. We are absolved with the words, "God, the Father of mercies, through the death and resurrection of his Son, has reconciled the world to himself and sent the Holy Spirit amongst us for the forgiveness of sins; through the ministry of the Church, may God give you pardon and peace, and I absolve you from your sins, in the name of the Father, and of the Son, and of the Holy Spirit."

Anointing of the sick heals, strengthens, or comforts the dying, the sick, or the elderly. Anointing of the sick sanctifies the soul and heals the body. The priest anoints a person with blessed oil and prays over him or her. If the person is dying, the priest will give him or her the Eucharist. This last Eucharist is called Viaticum. This Latin word refers to Jesus' being a fellow traveler with a person on his or her final journey.

Holy Orders is the sacrament by which persons are ordained (commissioned) and empowered to preach the Word of God and to administer the sacraments. There are orders (ranks) of ministry, or service, in the Church: deacons, priests, and bishops. With the consent of the people of God, the bishop lays his hands upon the person seeking ordination and says a prayer. The character of holy orders is the person's permanent commitment to the sacramental priesthood.

Matrimony is the sacrament in which God blesses and strengthens the love of a man and **a woman.** They confer this sacrament on each other and become husband and wife. The two pledge themselves to each other in a permanent union for the rest of their lives. The priest officiates at the wedding and is the official witness of the Church.

5 What Catholics believe about the Church

Membership

The Church is the people of God (men, women, and children) who acknowledge God as their creator and Jesus as their savior. They strive to love God and their fellow human beings as Jesus commanded. The Church is the "faithful of the whole world." Jesus founded the Church on Peter and the apostles. Thus, Jesus' work of redeeming people has continued through the ages and has spread around the whole world.

Sometimes the Church is called the Mystical Body of Christ. Each one of us is a part of Christ's body, and he is the head. The Holy Spirit is called the soul of the Church.

The term *communion of saints* refers to the entire community of faithful. It refers to the faithful in heaven, to the faithful in purgatory, and to the faithful on earth. The dead and the living are parts or members of Christ's Body.

Saints are men and women who have lived the Christian life—loved God and neighbor—in an extraordinary or heroic way. They are models of Christian living. Over the centuries the Church has declared certain men and women to be saints. As a result, they deserve our veneration. This means we can pray to them so that they will pray to God for us. Sometimes Mary is referred to as the greatest of the saints.

The mission or purpose of the Church is to sanctify men and women. In other words, the Church seeks to make them holy by proclaiming the Good News of Jesus, by teaching the commandments to love God and neighbor, and by conferring God's love through the grace of the sacraments.

Responsibilities

There are certain rules that members of the Church must obey. Members of the Catholic Church must believe in God, strive to love God and their neighbors, follow the example and teachings of Jesus, and observe the laws of the Church.

Church law requires Catholics to attend Mass on Sundays and Holy Days and to observe the rules of fast and abstinence on Ash Wednesday, Good Friday, and on other Fridays during Lent.

Catholics must receive the sacrament of reconciliation if they have committed a mortal sin, and they must receive the Eucharist during the Easter season. Catholics are also required to support the Church through financial contributions.

There are six Holy Days in the United States:

> The Solemnity of Mary, Mother of God (January 1)
>
> The Ascension of Jesus into heaven (Fortieth day after Easter)
>
> The Assumption of Mary into heaven (August 15)
>
> All Saints' Day (November 1)
>
> Immaculate Conception (December 8)
>
> Christmas (December 25)

Fasting is a form of self-denial. Abstinence is refraining from eating meat. Persons who fast cut down on, or limit, their eating. They eat one full meal and two smaller meals a day, enough to maintain their strength. Fasting is done to encourage spiritual growth, to control appetites, to imitate Jesus in his Passion, and to make up for sins committed.

Life

Prayer is our response to the presence of God in our lives.
Prayer is a conversation with God or a
message that we address to God. There
are different kinds of prayer. In a prayer of
petition we ask God for what we need or
want. In prayers of praise and thanksgiving
we adore and thank God for the many gifts
and blessings we enjoy. Meditation, or
reflection, leads to prayer. A popular form
of meditation is the rosary. The Divine Office,
a collection of readings from Scripture, is
communal daily prayer.

Liturgy is the official public prayer of the Church. Liturgy
consists of celebrating the Eucharist and the
other sacraments, praying the Divine Office,
and carrying out the ceremonies of the
Church.

**The liturgical year is divided into two seasons: Christmas
and Easter.** The Christmas season is

preceded by Advent. Advent is a season
during which we prepare for the coming of
our redeemer. The Christmas season begins
on Christmas and ends on Epiphany. The
Easter season is preceded by Lent. Lent
begins on Ash Wednesday. Lent is a season
during which we do penance. The Easter
season begins on Easter and ends on
Pentecost. The rest of the liturgical year is
called "ordinary time." During ordinary time
there are many saints' days, or feasts that
honor the saints.

Organization

The Church is made up of nearly two thousand local churches, or dioceses. Various parishes make up a diocese. The spiritual leader of a diocese is the bishop. Bishops around the world are in communion, or have a bonding relationship, with each other and with the pope (bishop of Rome). The pope is the Vicar of Christ, the head of the Church on earth. He is the spiritual leader of all the bishops, priests, and faithful who are in communion with him.

The word *catholic* means universal or undivided. At one time the Church was truly catholic or undivided. It was under the leadership of the pope in Rome. But since that time two great divisions have occurred within the Church.

The first great division within the Church occurred in 1054 c.e. Sometimes it is called the Eastern Schism. The word *schism* means a separation or rip. In that year, the churches in the western and eastern parts of the old Roman empire separated from each other. We call the churches of the west the Roman Catholic Church. The bishops of the west regard the pope as their spiritual leader. We call the churches of the east the Eastern Orthodox Church. The bishops of the east regard the patriarch (bishop) of Constantinople (Istanbul) as their spiritual leader.

Later on, some of the churches of the East once again entered into communion with the pope. We call these churches Eastern Catholic (Uniate) Churches. The Eastern Catholic Churches have retained their own traditions and liturgy.

The second great division within the Church began in 1517 c.e. It was a division within the Roman Catholic Church. It is called the Reformation. In that year Martin Luther (a German monk) attacked corruption in the Church. He called upon the Church to reform itself. Many people were attracted to his ideas. They looked to Luther and to others like him for leadership. Soon new churches were formed throughout Europe. Disagreements within these churches led to the formation of other churches.

In 1570 c.e., a smaller division occurred within the Roman Catholic Church. Queen Elizabeth I of England was excommunicated by Pius V in the Papal Bull, *Regnans Excelsis*. As a result, the Church of England came into existence with its own spiritual leader, the archbishop of Canterbury. The churches in communion with the See of Canterbury are called the Anglican Communion. These churches claim that there are three branches of the ancient church: Catholic (Rome), Orthodox (Istanbul), and Anglican (Canterbury).